Girl ✸ Talk

Questions and Answers About Daily Dramas, Disasters, and Delights

by Nancy Loewen and Paula Skelley

illustrated by Julissa Mora

Content adviser:
John E. Desrochers, PhD

CAPSTONE YOUNG READERS
a capstone imprint

Table of Contents

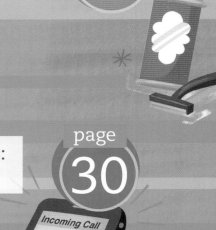

Isabella

Lan

Claudia

Sagal

Got questions about growing up?
About friends, family, or school?

We've got answers!

We know what you're going through. We've been there! If you find our advice helpful—great! And if there are some things you can't quite work through on your own, talk to a trusted adult. Parents, teachers, and school counselors are ready to help.

Tangles, Growth Spurts, and Being You

Questions and Answers About Growing Up

What's the best part of growing up?

Is it that you get to do more things on your own? That your allowance gets bigger? That you start looking less like a little kid and more like an adult?

Or that you can make more of your own decisions?

For all the great parts of growing up, there are just as many confusing parts. **GROWING UP IS ABOUT CHANGE— LOTS OF IT!**

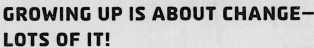

One day you're playing dress up, and the next you're wearing a bra. Your moods are all over the place, and sometimes you wish everybody would just **LEAVE YOU ALONE.**

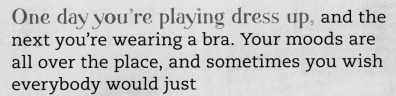

What do YOU want to know about growing up?

5

Changing Bodies

Q I've been hearing the word "puberty" a lot lately. What does puberty mean?

A Puberty is when your body begins to change from child to adult. For girls that means your breasts will start to develop, and hair will grow under your arms and in your pubic area. You'll get taller. Your body will start to fill out and change shape. And you'll start getting your period.

Puberty doesn't happen all at once. It takes place over a number of years. Some girls start puberty at 8 or 9. Others are 12 or older. Every girl has her own timeline. Your body will know when it's the right time for you.

Q What is B.O.?

A B.O. stands for body odor.

You've heard of hormones, right? Hormones basically tell the body what to do. Hormones also make your sweat glands go a little crazy—especially the ones under your arms. The sweat mixes with bacteria, and that's where the smell comes from.

You can avoid B.O. by taking a bath or shower every day. If you play sports or are just really active, you might even need to bathe twice. You should also use deodorant or antiperspirant. What's the difference? Antiperspirant keeps you from producing sweat, while deodorant battles the bacteria. (Most antiperspirants include a little deodorant too—just in case.)

Q My mom has never talked to me about puberty. How do I get up the courage to ask her questions?

A It's hard to talk about this stuff, especially if your mom hasn't brought it up yet. Instead of sitting down for a big formal talk, ask questions while you're doing other things. Some kids and parents have good talks in the car. After a while you'll both get used to the idea that you're old enough to ask these questions. Your conversations should get easier. But if not, it's OK to talk to another trusted adult.

Tip Clip

Some kids put on weight right before a growth spurt. Not a big deal. Eat healthy, sleep well, and the rest will take care of itself.

Some of my friends wear bras, but I'm nowhere near being ready for one. Should I get one anyway?

A That's up to you. Some girls can't wait to wear a bra. Others want to put it off as long as they can. You could try one and see what you think. There are cotton bras that feel like T-shirts, which might be a good way to get started. Maybe some days you wear a bra and some days you don't! It's your body and your decision.

Q My friend looks like she needs to wear a bra. Should I say something?

 There's a good chance your friend already knows she needs to wear a bra. Maybe she's embarrassed to talk to an adult about it. Have a friend-to-friend talk and find out what she's thinking.

If she really doesn't realize she needs a bra and goes too long without wearing one, she could get teased about it. And you don't want that to happen. In that case it's better for you to say something. Part of being a good friend is talking about all kinds of things, even if they might make you uncomfortable. But remember, no matter what you think, she's the one who has to feel OK with her choices.

A few of the boys in my class tease the girls who wear bras, including me. It's so embarrassing. What should we do?

 Don't be embarrassed. The changes you and your girlfriends are going through happen to everyone eventually. Ignore the boys. If they don't stop, tell your teacher. He or she can help sort it out.

The boys themselves may be uncomfortable about growing up. Teasing you might be a way of trying to cover up their feelings. That's not an excuse, though.

 My dad and I can talk about almost anything, but I'm worried about talking to him about bras and stuff like that.

 Your dad might be more nervous than you are! Both of you are changing. You're the one growing up, but your dad has new challenges as a parent too. You're lucky, because you already have a good relationship with him. If you both get a little embarrassed, that's OK. It will get easier each time you talk.

Q How old do you have to be to shave your legs?

A That depends on how old you are when you WANT to shave your legs, and when your parents say it's OK. Shaving your legs is a choice. Not everyone does. In some countries, women don't shave at all.

Maybe you've heard that your hair will grow back thicker and darker. It won't. It just looks that way because you're seeing the blunt ends of the hair.

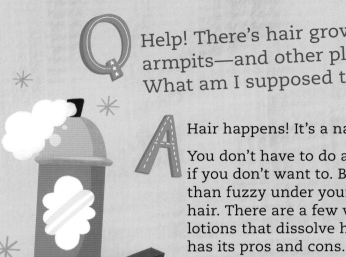

Q Help! There's hair growing in my armpits—and other places too. What am I supposed to do about it?

A Hair happens! It's a natural part of growing up.

You don't have to do anything about underarm hair if you don't want to. But if you'd rather go smooth than fuzzy under your arms, you can remove the hair. There are a few ways to do that: shaving, lotions that dissolve hair, and waxing. Each method has its pros and cons. Talk to your mom or another adult you trust. Before you actually try anything, be sure you have a parent's permission.

Q Shaving under my arms scares me. What if I cut myself?

A Shaving can be a little scary at first. But don't worry. If you do cut yourself, it will just sting a little, and the cut will heal quickly.

There are a lot of things you can do to prevent cuts. First, pick a razor that's specially designed to prevent nicks and cuts. Use plenty of soap or shaving cream. Don't press too hard, and rinse the razor often.

If you use an electric razor, the blades won't ever touch your skin directly. Electric razors don't shave as closely as other razors do, but you for sure won't cut yourself.

Q I've grown 3 inches this year and wear a bra. Everything about my body seems different and strange. I wish I could go back in time and just be a kid again.

A A lot of girls feel this way. One day you're carefree and confident, and the next day you're tripping over your own feet. It's so confusing! But hang in there. The main thing is to accept yourself as you are, right now. You may feel awkward for a while, but in time you'll get used to the new you.

And you don't have to change the way you act just because your body is different. If you want to snuggle up next to your mom, go ahead. If you feel like watching a scary movie with friends, that's OK too.

The girls on my bus sometimes whisper about "periods." I know they don't mean the little dot at the end of a sentence! Where can I go to get the right information about periods?

 You're smart to ask about the RIGHT information. Sometimes kids don't get all their facts straight, and they spread all sorts of wild ideas. First step: Talk to your mom or another woman you know well. Some of the information gets a little technical, so it's OK to do some research at the library. If there's anything you don't understand, ask an adult to explain it.

Tip Clip

Keep a travel-size deodorant in your backpack. If you forget to put on deodorant at home in the morning, you'll be covered!

Hair and Skin Care

Q My mom wants me to cut my hair. I don't want to. Ever! Why can't I just let it grow?

A Long hair can be so pretty. But even long hair needs a little TLC to keep it healthy. Get a trim at least once every few months to avoid split ends.

Tell your mom why you like your hair long. Then ask why she wants you to cut it. Do you have trouble taking care of your long hair? Does it get in the way when you play sports? Try to find a compromise that works for both of you.

Q I need to wash my hair a lot more often than I used to. It gets greasy so fast! What's going on?

A Greasy hair is no fun. But it's part of growing up. Here's what's going on: At the base of every hair is a tiny oil gland. We need a little oil to keep our hair from getting too dry and breaking. But during puberty, our oil glands sometimes go overboard and make too much oil. That's why you need to wash your hair more often. So keep the shampoo bottle handy.

What causes pimples? And how do I keep from getting them?

Pimples are the worst! But almost every kid gets them at some point. Adults can get them too.

Pimples form when pores (those tiny holes in our skin) get clogged with oil, dead skin cells, and bacteria. To keep your pores clear, gently wash your face once or twice a day with warm water and mild soap. And try not to touch your face during the day, especially if you do have a few pimples. Picking at them or squeezing them will just make them worse.

If your face breaks out a lot, ask your mom or dad to help you find the right skincare products.

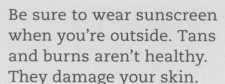 Tip Clip

Be sure to wear sunscreen when you're outside. Tans and burns aren't healthy. They damage your skin.

Appearance

Q I'm bigger than all my friends. And I don't just mean that I'm taller. What should I do when kids tease me about being overweight? Sometimes even my best friends say things that hurt my feelings.

A People come in all shapes and sizes. Just look around. Let your friends know that you don't judge them by their size, and they shouldn't judge you by yours either. Be clear and direct. Your friends might not realize how hurtful they're being.

What should you do if other kids tease you? Ignore them, change the subject, or leave. If the teasing gets really bad, and they won't stop, tell an adult. That's bullying, and you shouldn't have to deal with bullying by yourself.

Remember, your weight is just one part of you. It's not the whole picture. Be strong, believe in yourself, and be proud of who you are.

Q I need to get braces on my teeth soon. Do braces hurt? I'm kind of freaked out.

A Lots of kids get braces to fix their teeth. No need to freak out. Braces can be a hassle, but you'll get used to them quickly. Your teeth may be sore for a few days right after you get them. Stick with soft foods, like macaroni or yogurt, until they feel better. About once a month, you'll get your braces adjusted. Your teeth may hurt a bit again for a day or so. The orthodontist will answer all of your questions and teach you how to take care of your braces.

Having braces will be worth it in the end. Keep picturing the amazing smile you'll have when the braces come off!

Q A couple of girls in my class told me they're going on a diet. I'm not overweight, but should I go on a diet too?

A Don't fall for all the dieting hype. Kids shouldn't go on diets unless a doctor tells them to. Being healthy is what's important. Right now you're growing the body you'll have for life. So take care of it. Eat fruits, vegetables, whole grains, and lean meats. Drink plenty of water. Try to get about an hour of exercise each day. Walk the dog, bike to your friend's house, or go inline skating with your cousins. If you live in a healthy way, you'll be at the right weight for you.

Q My eye doctor says I need glasses, but I'm scared I won't like the way I look. I want to get contacts but my dads think I'm too young.

A Most kids are nervous about getting their first pair of glasses. It's a big change. Think of shopping for glasses like shopping for another accessory—say, a scarf or earrings. Take your time picking out your frames. Try on different styles and colors. See how they look with your hair and face shape. Glasses can add to your fab style. If possible, get more than one pair, so you can switch off according to your mood.

Contacts take longer to adjust to and are a lot more work, so listen to your dads on that one. If you still want contacts when you're older, you can talk about it then.

A few of the girls in my class have started to wear mascara and eye shadow. What's the right age to start wearing makeup?

 That depends on how your parents feel about makeup. Before you buy or start using makeup, talk to them. Everybody's family is different.

Most girls don't start wearing makeup until middle school. Or they wear it for a special occasion, like a dance recital or play. Some girls keep it simple, starting with just a little lip gloss.

There's no rule that says girls or women HAVE to wear makeup. To some people, it feels weird. Others think makeup makes them look more like themselves. Figure out what works best for you. But there's no need to hurry. You've got plenty of time.

Tip Clip

Don't let others push you into shaving, wearing makeup, dressing in a certain way, or anything like that. Your body—your call.

Q Why do boys in my class act like little kids? Why can't they act their age?

A Girls develop earlier than boys—mentally and physically. So right now the differences between boys and girls can seem huge! Be patient. And remember that growing up is just as awkward and confusing for boys as it is for girls. In time the boys will catch up.

Q A few of the girls in my class have boyfriends. They talk about going on dates and kissing. I've had crushes on boys, but I wouldn't want to kiss them! Is there something wrong with me?

A Lots of girls feel the way you do! Some girls think that having a boyfriend makes them cool. But it's not cool to do anything you're not ready for. Plus, you don't know how much of what they're saying is true. Some or all of it could be made up.

People have different ideas of what it means to date. Some kids go on group dates. Boys and girls will all go together to a movie, a bowling alley, or someplace like that. Many parents want kids to wait to date until they're in high school. Others are OK driving their kids to the movies and letting it be a "date."

When it comes to boyfriends and dating, it doesn't really matter what others do. It's up to you and your family.

The boy who moved in next door is super cute! But whenever I see him, I freeze and don't know what to say. What should I do?

 Funny how a super-cute boy can leave you tongue-tied, isn't it? But he's no different from anyone else. How do you usually get to know people? You probably talk about what you like to do. You see if you have things in common and if you enjoy being around each other. Do those same things now.

It's OK to feel nervous. Once you take the first step and start talking to him, you'll feel more confident. If you don't have anything in common, it doesn't matter how cute he is. Friendships and relationships should be based on more than looks.

Tip Clip

Do you sometimes think boys are from a different planet? If you need advice about boys, don't just ask your mom. Include your dad or other male relatives in the conversation. You might learn a lot.

Q I think I should be able to spend my allowance however I want. My parents don't agree. What do you think?

A Every family has different values and rules when it comes to money. Ask your parents what they're worried about. Do they want you to save your money? Do they think you would waste money on things they wouldn't approve of?

See if you can work out a compromise. Maybe you could use part of your allowance the way you want, but let them put the rest in savings. Or you could alternate weeks. Keep talking with your parents, and you'll figure out a solution.

Q My mom wants to pick out all of my clothes. How can I convince her that I'm old enough to choose what I like?

A Tell your mom how you feel. Then find out where she's coming from. Does she really enjoy buying clothes for you? Is she worried about cost? Does she have strong ideas about what's OK and not OK for you to wear? Get it all out in the open.

You'll probably end up meeting somewhere in the middle—at least for now. She'll get to pick out some things, and you'll get to pick out some things. Whatever happens, try to have a good attitude. Shopping will be more fun that way!

Q My parents come into my room whenever they want. That used to be OK with me, but not anymore. How can I tell them that I want my room to feel like MY room?

 A Your parents are probably so used to coming into your room that they don't even think about it. Explain that you'd like more privacy. Ask them to knock first, or have certain hours when they know to leave you alone. In return they might ask you to follow certain rules, like bringing your own dirty clothes to the laundry room.

Keep in mind, it is still their house, but together you should be able to figure out a plan that works.

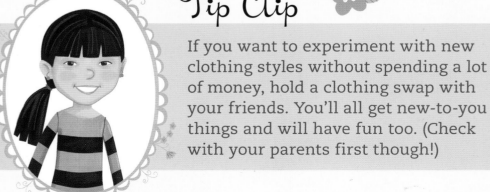

Tip Clip

If you want to experiment with new clothing styles without spending a lot of money, hold a clothing swap with your friends. You'll all get new-to-you things and will have fun too. (Check with your parents first though!)

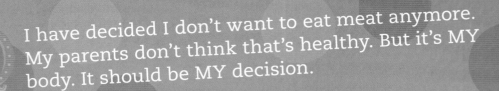

I have decided I don't want to eat meat anymore. My parents don't think that's healthy. But it's MY body. It should be MY decision.

It IS your body, but you're their kid, and they're responsible for making sure you get everything your body needs to grow. You can be a vegetarian and still be healthy—definitely! But you need to know what you're doing to get enough protein, iron, and other things. To your parents, going vegetarian—especially for just one person in the family—might seem like a lot of work. But you can make it easier for them if you do your research. There are tons of healthy, kid-friendly vegetarian recipes on the Internet. Many of them even include nutrition info. Or you could check out a recipe book at your library.

Are your parents concerned about cost? Pre-packaged vegetarian foods can be pricy. But if you learn to cook with vegetables, beans, rice, and whole grains, eating veggie can be cheaper than eating meat. Pitch in with the planning, cooking, and cleanup, and your parents might start seeing things your way.

Q I feel like a little kid when my parents hire a babysitter. I'm ready to stay home by myself. Why can't they see that?

A Sometimes parents have a hard time seeing that their kids are growing up. They just want to keep their kids safe, at any age, even if it means hiring a babysitter.

If you're serious about staying home alone, talk to your parents. See if you can have a trial run. Ask them to make a list of rules they expect you to follow and phone numbers to call in case of an emergency. If the trial run goes well, your parents might agree that you're ready to stay home alone.

Tip Clip

Don't judge other people's food choices. There are lots of reasons people eat or don't eat certain foods, including health issues or cultural traditions.

25

Plugged In

Q My friend wants me to go to a PG-13 movie with her. My moms don't want me to see PG-13 movies. Should I tell my friend I don't have permission? Or should I go and not tell my parents?

A Tell your friend you're not allowed to see PG-13 movies. She might be disappointed, but she'll understand. There must be more than one movie that you and your friend would like to see. Find one that your parents are OK with.

It can feel really unfair when other kids get to do things you're not allowed to. Just remember that your moms have good reasons for their rules. They know you and what you're ready for.

Why do I need a parent's permission to join a social media site? If the site's for kids, why can't I just sign up by myself?

The Internet is like its own universe. It's enormous! And it's easy to stumble onto things you wish you'd never seen or to be tricked into giving private information. Parents need to see for themselves that the sites you're going to are safe and at the right age level. The people who make social media sites for kids understand that. They want parents to trust them. Without that trust, the site wouldn't be able to exist. Sure, it's a little annoying to have to get your parents involved. But it's just to keep you safe.

Tip Clip

Online manners count! Don't say anything online that you wouldn't say in person.

What's wrong with having a computer or TV in my room? My parents won't let me have either one, and I don't think that's fair.

 There are lots of things on TV and the Internet that aren't kid-friendly. If TVs and computers are in a family area, it's easier for your parents to see what you're watching and make sure the programs are right for you.

It's easy to lose track of time when you're surfing the web or watching TV. Too much screen time isn't good for your brain or your body. Did you know you're supposed to stop your screen time at least an hour before going to bed? You'll sleep better if you do. Your parents' rule might not seem fair, but they're doing what they think is best for you.

My dad turns off the radio in the car when certain songs are on. I get annoyed, but he says some songs are bad. What can be so bad about a song on the radio?

 Movies have ratings that tell you if a movie is OK for kids. Think of your dad like a ratings monitor for songs on the radio. He knows that some songs have language or ideas he doesn't think you're old enough for yet. Your dad's just watching out for you and trying to do what's right. Maybe you could work together to make a playlist that everyone in your family would enjoy.

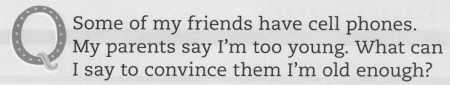 Some of my friends have cell phones. My parents say I'm too young. What can I say to convince them I'm old enough?

There's not much you can SAY, but there's plenty you can DO. Keep track of your things, help around the house without being asked, and follow the house rules. A cell phone is a big deal. It costs a lot of money. Your parents may worry that you'll lose it, break it, or run up a huge phone bill. Even if you do everything right, they might still say no. But if you earn their trust, they'll be more likely to say yes.

Tip Clip

It's good to unplug every so often. Spend a few days without your computer or tablet. Who knows what adventures you'll have!

Besties, Sleepovers, and Drama Queens

Questions and Answers About Friends

Who makes you laugh?

Who helps out when you're having a tough time? Who lends you a shoulder to cry on? Who accepts you for who you are and loves spending time with you?

Your friends!

Now that you're growing up, maybe you've noticed that your friends are becoming more and more important to you. Maybe you've also noticed that **FRIENDSHIPS TAKE A LOT OF WORK!** All friendships have their highs and lows. You might not always know the right thing to say or do. At times you might feel angry, confused, jealous, or even scared. Friendships grow and change—just like YOU grow and change.

What do YOU want to know about friends?

Friendship Basics

Q Last year I had a lot of friends in my class. This year I don't. How can I make new friends?

A Be brave and take the first step. Just start talking to other kids. And don't worry about being nervous! It's OK. Everyone feels that way, even the popular kids. Try asking questions about what you're working on in school. Compliment somebody, or help a classmate with an art project. Invite someone new to your house to do homework or hang out. Find kids who like the same things you do by joining a club or an after-school sport. Are there any kids who play the same video games or read the same kinds of books? Get to know them, and soon you'll have new friends.

Q How do I know if my friends really like me?

A Good question. Start by asking yourself if YOU are a good friend. Do you listen when your friends are talking? Are you happy when they get good news? Sad when they get bad news? Can they count on you to keep your promises? Then think about how your friends treat you. Are they doing all of these things? If you and your friends treat each other the way you would want to be treated, no worries!

Here's something else to think about: If you're always wondering if your friends like you, maybe you need to like yourself first. Are you perfect? No! But neither is anyone else. Accept yourself as you are, and your true friends will do the same.

There's a new girl joining our class next week. How can I make her feel welcome?

 Just start with "hello" and a friendly smile. One small word will make her feel welcome. Introduce yourself and a few friends too. Ask about her old school or her old neighborhood. Sit with her at lunch and invite her to join in at recess. Offer to help her with homework if she needs it. You could even invite her to get together after school.

Tip Clip

Be the type of friend you want to have, and you won't need to worry about having enough friends.

I'm confused. When is keeping secrets OK?

It's OK to keep secrets about things like surprise parties and gifts. Those are good secrets. But other secrets have to do with privacy—like if your friend tells you that she has a crush on someone. It might be tempting to tell other friends if they promise not to tell. But don't! You can't control what anyone else says, so keep your own lips zipped.

There are also secrets that make you feel bad inside. It's definitely not OK to keep those. If you have a secret that is hurting you or someone else, tell a parent or another trusted adult. They can help you do the right thing.

Q This year my best friend is part of the popular group. I don't fit in with her new friends. What should I do?

A Just because your friend is in a new group doesn't mean you're not still friends too. Don't treat her any differently or ask her to pick you over her other friends. Make sure she knows how important she is to you, but also spend time with other friends.

It's hard not to worry about who's popular and who's not. But don't stress out. Groups and friends change, but YOU don't have to change. Be yourself. Do the things you enjoy, and be happy with who you are.

Q Sometimes I don't want to be with my friends. I'd rather be by myself. Is something wrong with me?

A No. Sometimes we all need to hole up in our rooms and read or draw or listen to music or whatever. We're like batteries—we need to recharge! Just tell your friends you need some alone time, and you'll catch up with them later. They might feel the same way.

Tricky Situations

Q I went shopping with my friend, and she dared me to steal makeup. She took a lip gloss. I didn't take anything, but now she calls me "Chicken!" What should I do?

A First of all, she sure doesn't sound like a friend. Tell her you are scared and for good reason—stealing is a crime. She could be caught for shoplifting. Ask her to tell her mom or dad what she did. If she doesn't, let your parents know, so they can guide you. By telling, you aren't being a bad friend. You're helping her.

Don't ever let friends make you do anything that goes against your own sense of right and wrong. Stand up for what you believe in. Your friends should respect you for being true to yourself.

Q I found out my best friend's mom is really sick. My friend hasn't said anything to me. How can I help?

A Pick a time when the two of you are alone, and tell her that you know. Ask her how she is and how her mom is feeling. Let her know that you are there for her and will listen. But don't tell anyone else. It should be up to her to decide who to tell and when. Sometimes it takes people a while before they want to share bad news with others. Try to give your friend something to smile about every day—a joke, a homemade card, or maybe just a hug.

There's a girl in my neighborhood who has Down syndrome. I want to invite her to my birthday party, but I'm scared my other friends will make fun of her. What should I do?

 If you want to invite her, go for it! When the party starts, make a point of introducing your neighbor to your other friends. Include her in things, and set a good example. The rest of your friends should follow your lead. As the party goes on, check in with your neighbor once in a while to make sure things are going OK.

Tip Clip

Take a few moments and imagine what it would be like to be someone else. Really think it through. How would you want to be treated?

Handling Differences

Q My friend is very quiet. I'm not quiet at all. How can I get her to open up?

A Try talking a little less, and maybe your friend will talk a little more. There may be some awkward silence, and you might feel like you have to fill the silence—but don't. You'll get used to it. You might even like those extra moments to get your own thoughts together. It's like a seesaw. If you find a balance, then neither of you will feel like you're getting bumped off the edge.

The main thing is to respect each other. Being quiet or outgoing isn't right or wrong, it's just one of the ways we're different from each other.

 My friend can be loud and obnoxious. It's embarrassing! What should I do?

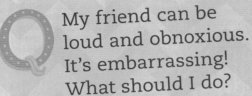 You don't need to feel embarrassed as long as YOU behave well. You and your friend are not the same person. Others will see that you're not the one doing those things.

If there are situations that really bother you, tell your friend how you feel, without being mean. Instead of saying, "You should do this" or "Stop doing that," use sentences that start with "I." Like, "I feel embarrassed when you talk so loud at the movies. Could you talk more quietly?"

No matter what you say, though, she gets to decide for herself how she'll behave. It's not up to you. What IS up to you is how you respond to her.

Tip Clip

It's great to "be yourself," but you need to let others be themselves too!

39

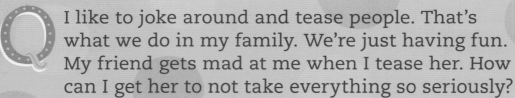 I like to joke around and tease people. That's what we do in my family. We're just having fun. My friend gets mad at me when I tease her. How can I get her to not take everything so seriously?

You should try to tone it down. Even if your teasing is just in fun, how your friend feels about it is what matters. You're not being a good friend if you keep ignoring her feelings.

Explain that you don't mean to hurt her feelings. Describe what your family is like, so she understands. Give her examples of things your family teases you about and why you don't let them get to you. Tell her you only tease people you care about!

Q My friends play a lot of sports. They're always talking about games and practices. How do I keep my friends if I'm not into sports?

A Focus on the things you have in common. People have more than one interest, right? If you like reading, talk about books. If you like art, create something cool together. If you like video games, invite them to your house to play. If you were friends before sports became important, there is no reason you can't be friends now.

Tip Clip

Bullying is different than teasing. When you bully, you are trying to hurt someone with your words or actions.

Dealing with Rejection

Q Some days my friends forget to save me a place to sit by them at lunch. This makes me sad AND mad. Should I tell them how I feel?

A Yes. It can be hard to tell friends that they've hurt your feelings. But if you don't tell them, you'll just get mad, and then your friendship may start to fall apart. Being honest makes friendships stronger.

Your friends probably aren't trying to be mean. They might just be thinking about other things. Chances are, they don't even know you're upset! Talk it through. If you expect them to save you a seat, say so, and do the same for them.

 I moved to a new state. My best friend from back home always wants to talk on the phone. But I have lots of new friends now. How can I let her know that I don't think we're best friends anymore?

That's tough. No matter how she finds out, she's going to be hurt. And that's sad. Sometimes we hurt people we care about even when we're not doing anything wrong.

Try to schedule your calls, so you both know what to expect. Or e-mail or text instead. Ask about fun things she's done. If she asks about your friendship, say, "You will always be my best friend from where I used to live. That will never change." Just saying "You're not my best friend anymore" would hurt too much. Give her time to find a new BFF.

Tip Clip

Turn challenges into opportunities. For example, if you can't sit by your friends at lunch, don't worry about it. Talk to the kids next to you and make new friends.

All of my friends were invited to Lola's birthday party, but I wasn't. They talk about the upcoming party all the time, and it makes me feel terrible. Should I say something to them?

 Yes, talk to your friends. They might not realize how bad you feel.

It's hard to be left out. But we can't all be included every time. Remind yourself that the party will be over soon. Then your friends will have other things to talk about. Make special plans with your family on that day so you'll have something to look forward to.

 My friend and I do lots of things together, but I'm always the one calling her—she never calls me. Does that mean she doesn't want to be my friend?

 Do you get along when you're together? If you do there might be other reasons she's not calling you. Some parents have strict rules about using the phone. Or maybe she doesn't call you because you always beat her to it. Tell her that it bothers you. Say that you would feel better if she called you once in a while.

My friend and I have been on the same soccer team forever. Now she made the traveling team, but I didn't. What if she doesn't want to be my friend anymore?

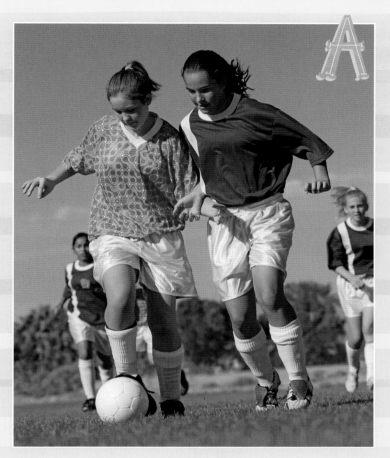

 You're probably dealing with lots of feelings right now. You're happy for your friend, disappointed for yourself, and maybe a little jealous too. Just keep treating your friend the way you always have. Focus on the things you like to do together. Who knows, you might be on the same team again someday.

If you and your friend do grow apart, though, you'll be OK. Some friendships last forever, and others don't. No matter what, our friends help make us who we are, and that's cool.

 Tip Clip

Friendships have ups and downs. A few bad days—or even weeks—don't mean your friendship is over.

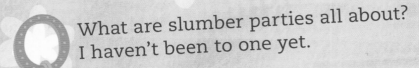

Q What are slumber parties all about? I haven't been to one yet.

A Every slumber party is different. It depends on the house, friends, parents, and rules. You might watch movies or play video games or paint your nails or share secrets. Or you might do all of those things! You might sit down at a table for a meal or just snack all night.

Here are some tips for having a great time:

Be nice to everyone. Don't leave anyone out.

Don't gossip about kids who aren't there. You wouldn't want kids talking about you behind your back, would you?

If you get tired and want to sleep, say so. You probably won't be the only one.

Clean up any messes you make.

Follow the rules. If the parents say, "Lights out at midnight," be sure to listen.

Fair warning: You might all experience some major crabbiness due to lack of sleep!

My friend asked me to a slumber party, but I don't like staying over at other people's homes. How do I tell her no?

 You're not alone—a lot of kids don't like sleeping over at other people's homes. Just tell your friends that you have to leave at a certain time, and leave it at that. If they bug you about it, be honest and say you sleep better in your own bed. If you miss out on something really fun, be a good sport about it.

 My friends Jessica and Hattie don't like each other. I feel stuck in the middle. Help!

 That's tricky! Tell them that if they say mean things about each other, you aren't going to listen. Then stick to it. Don't try to make them like each other. That will put you in the middle for sure. If things get tense, change the subject or start doing something new.

Tip Clip

Do your friends gossip? You don't have to join in. Ask them to stop. Or just keep changing the subject until they get it.

Handling Conflict

 Q Two girls on my bus say bad things about me. They make the other kids laugh at me. Sometimes they pass around mean notes. I hate riding the bus now! How can I get them to stop?

A These girls are bullies. Do your best to ignore them. Act calm and confident, even if you don't feel that way inside. Sit with a friend. Or sit up front by the bus driver. If you sit on the right side of the bus, the driver can see you better.

You should also tell your bus driver, parents, and teacher. Your school has rules about bullying. These girls are breaking the rules big-time. Don't worry, telling on them doesn't mean you're a tattletale. It means you're brave, strong, and willing to stick up for yourself.

 Q My friend is mad at me, but I don't know why. She won't tell me what I did. How can we get back to being friends?

 A If you've asked her why she's mad, and she won't tell you, it's her problem now, isn't it? Tell her that whatever it was, you didn't mean to upset her. Say that you want to go back to being friends. Then drop the subject and do the things you always do. Eventually she'll figure out that holding on to anger isn't much fun.

I made up some stuff to sound cool around the popular girls. Now I'm afraid they'll find out I lied. Should I tell them the truth?

 Yes. If they find out from someone else, they won't ever believe you. Telling them the truth won't be easy, but it's the right thing to do. It will be the first step toward rebuilding trust.

You also need to be honest with yourself about why you lied in the first place. Do you feel like you're not good enough as you are? Instead of making up stories that aren't true, learn to know—and like—the real you!

Tip Clip

Make a habit of being nice—even to people who aren't your friends. Everyone deserves to be treated with kindness.

Q I said something mean to my friend. I wish I could take it back. How do I make things better?

 **A** A face-to-face apology is best. If you're too nervous for that, you could text or e-mail your friend. Listen to her if she wants to talk. You don't need to keep apologizing, but let her know she's important to you. It might take a long time before she trusts you again. But keep treating her like a good friend, and maybe one day you'll be good friends again.

 Q My friend lies to her parents all the time. I don't like it. What should I say to her?

A Be honest with your friend. Tell her that lying makes you uncomfortable. And it's wrong. Let her know that lying will hurt your friendship. Tell her it's hard for you to believe her because you've heard her lie so many times.

If she keeps on lying, you'll need to think hard about your friendship. Is she really the kind of friend you want to have?

I got a new haircut, then my friend got the same haircut. I got a pair of pink shoes, then she started wearing pink shoes! How can I keep her from copying me?

 If someone copies you, it's because she wants to be like you. If she wants to be like you, she must think you're pretty great!

If you want her to stop, though, you need to say something. Tell her that it makes you feel weird when she does the same things you do. Be sure to compliment her on the things she does that are different from you. Maybe her self-confidence needs a boost.

I like to wear clothes that aren't like everyone else's. I love having my own look. But my friends tease me about it all the time. What should I do?

 It's great to be an individual. But if you want to stand out from the crowd, expect that others will have something to say about your look. If the teasing is good-natured, do your best to ignore it. But if the teasing really hurts your feelings, tell your friends and ask them to stop.

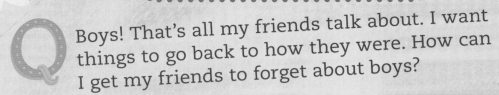

Boys

Q Boys! That's all my friends talk about. I want things to go back to how they were. How can I get my friends to forget about boys?

A That might not be possible! If you feel uncomfortable, try changing the subject. You can spend more time with other friends who aren't quite so boy crazy. But be prepared—your own attitude toward boys might change one day.

Q My best friend and I like the same boy. What should we do?

A Girlfriends are too important to lose. Don't be mean or do anything you might feel sorry about later. You don't want to lose the friend you have by trying to get the boy you don't have. If the boy likes one of you, be a good sport about it. Who knows, pretty soon you might like a different boy anyway!

Q The girls and boys in my class call each other boyfriend and girlfriend. Sometimes they hold hands. I think it's gross. Is there something wrong with me? What is having a boyfriend all about?

A Don't worry, nothing is wrong with you. In some cultures, girls can't hold hands with boys until they're grown up and married.

Having a "boyfriend" means different things to different people. Maybe it's just two kids saying that they like each other. Or maybe the boy and girl hang out together or talk on the phone, just like regular friends. The important thing to know is that you don't HAVE to have a boyfriend.

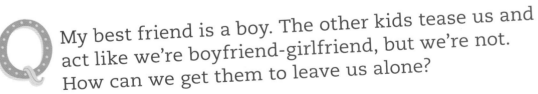

Q My best friend is a boy. The other kids tease us and act like we're boyfriend-girlfriend, but we're not. How can we get them to leave us alone?

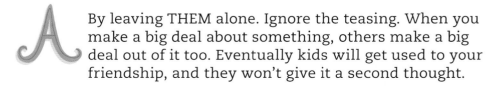

A By leaving THEM alone. Ignore the teasing. When you make a big deal about something, others make a big deal out of it too. Eventually kids will get used to your friendship, and they won't give it a second thought.

Friends and Family

Q My best friend is allowed to wear makeup, get her ears pierced, AND watch PG-13 movies. My parents won't let me do any of those things! How can my friend and I stay friends when our families are so different?

A As long as your friend respects your family's rules, you should get along fine. Do the things that bring you and your friend together. Don't waste time worrying about the things that might pull you apart.

As you grow up, your parents will change their rules based on what they feel is right for your age. Talk with them about the rules. That way you'll understand the reasons behind them.

Q My friend gets mad about things that aren't my fault—like if my mom won't allow an overnight or a movie. I'm already feeling bad, and when my friend gets mad I feel even worse. How should I handle this?

A Just tell your friend how you feel. She might not realize how unfair she's being. Sometimes people get mad because they don't know how to deal with their own bad feelings. That's no excuse for how she's treating you, but it might help you understand her better. It's OK to tell her, "We'll talk later," if being around her upsets you.

I have a friend who's really rich. I'm not. I would be embarrassed to have her come to my house. What can I tell her when she wants to come over?

Say yes! You don't need to feel embarrassed. MOST people aren't rich. Remember, you are a worthwhile person no matter what your family has or doesn't have.

If your friend is really a friend, she will accept you as you are. If she comes over and decides she doesn't want to be your friend anymore, then she wasn't your friend to begin with.

 My friend's family serves food that I've never tried before. Her grandparents speak a different language. Everything's so different from what I'm used to! What should I do?

 If you avoid going to her house, sooner or later it will affect your friendship. Try to find ways to feel more comfortable when you're there. Ask your friend to teach you a few basic words in her grandparents' language, like "hello," "please," and "thank you." Ask your friend questions about her family's history and culture. If trying new foods is a problem for you, ask for just a small taste to start with. Be friendly and respectful. Soon your friend's house won't seem strange at all.

Tip Clip

If you want respect, you need to show respect—not just to your friends but to your friends' families too. After all, you want them to respect YOUR family, don't you?

Siblings, Curfews, and How to Deal

Questions and Answers About Family Life

What do you think of when you hear the word *"family"?*

Do you think of brothers or sisters? One parent or two? How about grandparents, aunts, uncles, and cousins? Maybe you think of your dog or hamster as part of the family. Families come in all shapes and sizes. No two are exactly alike. But the one thing they all have is love.

Families aren't always easy.

Just when you think you've got things figured out, something changes. Brothers and sisters get on your nerves. Parents divorce or remarry or have more kids. Grandparents get sick or move away.

SOMETIMES YOU DON'T WANT ANYTHING TO DO WITH YOUR FAMILY.

 At other times you can't wait to tell them about your day.

What do YOU want to know about family life?

Q Lately I'd rather talk to my mom than my dad. Is that OK?

A Sure! Just because you have more to say to your mom right now doesn't mean you love your dad any less. It might be easier to talk about things like clothes or body changes or girlfriend troubles with your mom. She's been through it. But you should still find ways to connect with your dad. Work on a project together. Or have a dad-and-daughter date at a special restaurant. Maybe one day it'll be easier to talk to your dad about some things than your mom. That's OK too. People grow and change and so do their relationships.

Q What should I do when my dad tells me to do one thing and my mom tells me to do something else?

A It's confusing when parents aren't on the same page. But it happens in every family at one time or another. Let your parents know they told you different things. Then give them a chance to work it out. Don't just follow whichever instructions you like better.

If your parents aren't around to set things straight, you'll have to decide for yourself. Trust your instincts and make the best decision you can, but talk to your parents as soon as possible.

Do these mix-ups happen a lot? Do your mom and dad always argue about parenting stuff? Ask them to write down their rules or find a better way to let you know what's going on.

If my parents aren't home, I can't have friends over. Not even my next-door neighbor! How can I convince my parents that the house won't fall down just because they aren't there?

Ask your parents to make a list of the things you need to do in order to have a friend over while they are out. Prove to them that you are responsible by following the family rules. Do you clean up after yourself? Do you let the dog out? Do you turn off lights and close windows and put food away and all that? Do you know who to call if something goes wrong?

See if your parents will say yes to a few "practice runs." Let them decide how long you and your friend can be alone. If everything goes OK, they may change their rules.

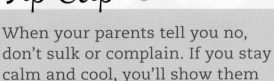 ## Tip Clip

When your parents tell you no, don't sulk or complain. If you stay calm and cool, you'll show them that you're growing up.

Q If I wash the car, my dad points out a spot I missed. If I get a B+, he says I should have tried harder to get an A. Sometimes I feel like I can't do anything right!

A Your dad wants you to be the best you can be. He probably doesn't realize that his comments aren't helping you do better—they're discouraging you from trying. Be honest and calmly tell him how you feel. Be honest with yourself too. If you aren't putting in a good effort, admit it.

Maybe your dad will get it. Maybe he won't. But if you know that you did your best, you can be proud of yourself no matter what.

Q My mom went back to work, and now everything is different. I have a lot more chores, and I can't do as many activities because she can't pick me up. Why can't she be just a mom again?

A Because she's not JUST a mom. She's a person too!

Is she working because your family needs the money? Is she working because she loves what she does? Either way, she's doing what she needs to do. Sure, change is tough, but you'll get used to it in time.

If there's a certain activity you really want to keep doing, see if your dad or an aunt or uncle can drive you. Or ask your parents to look into carpooling.

Q My dad is awesome, but I'm embarrassed to bring my friends home because he doesn't speak English. What should I do?

¡Hola! Hello!

A You already said your dad's awesome, so really, what's there to be embarrassed about? Bridge the gap between your dad and your friends. Teach him some basic words to say to your friends. Ask him to teach you and your friends some things to say in his language. Just seeing you and your dad together will help your friends see how great he is—even if they don't speak the same language.

61

Q My parents are super busy. It's like they never have time to do anything fun as a family. Any suggestions?

A Tell your parents you want more family time. Once they know how important it is to you, maybe they'll cut back on some of their other activities.

Keep a list of fun things you can do together that don't take a lot of time. How about a quick game of cards, a bike ride, or a picnic supper in the park? How about watching funny YouTube videos? Or pick some "family only" days every month—everyone agrees not to make other plans on those days.

Even ordinary tasks can be fun if everyone's got the right attitude. Go grocery shopping together. Wash the car. Paint the living room! It's about spending time together, not what you do.

I wish I could spend more time with my mom, without my little brother tagging along. Is there anything I can do about it?

 Little brothers and sisters are great, but so is time alone with your mom. It might take some planning though. Talk to your mom about ways to find more "girl time" together. Plan an at-home mani-pedi during one of his naps. Invite your mom to watch a movie with you after your little brother goes to bed for the night. Maybe your brother could have some special time with another family member while you have time with your mom.

Q How do I tell my parents they've scheduled me for too many activities?

A Decide which activities are the most important to you. What do you enjoy most? Make a list of the reasons you chose them. If you think it through, your parents will know you are serious and not just having a bad week. Pick a time when you can talk without being interrupted. Explain that you're feeling stressed out and need to cut back on your activities. Who knows, they might like having more time at home too.

Q My sister has ADHD and never gets around to doing things she's supposed to do. Why do I have to be responsible when she doesn't have to be?

A Having ADHD means that her brain works differently than yours does. It's a big challenge to make herself do things she's not interested in (like helping around the house). Your sister probably wishes she were more like you. Be proud of how responsible you are. Don't worry about what she's doing or not doing—that's between your sister and your parents. One thing you CAN do is encourage her. Tell her she did a great job cleaning her room. Ask if she will help you do the dishes. Doing chores together might help her stay focused on what needs to be done. She'll try harder if she feels her family is on her side.

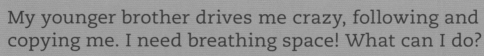

Q My younger brother drives me crazy, following and copying me. I need breathing space! What can I do?

A That doesn't sound like much fun for either of you! Instead of always trying to get away from your brother, give him some of your time. Tell him you'll play a game with him, but when you're done playing, you'll get to do your own thing. Or set up a "playdate," just like you would if he were a friend and not your little brother. When the playdate is over, you get time to yourself. Try to stick to a routine, so he'll know what to expect. And if your brother still gets in your way too much, ask your parents for help.

How can I stop fighting with my brother and sister?

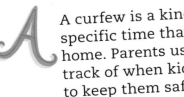

Arguing can become a habit. A bad habit! To break it, pay attention to your thoughts and feelings. Are you mad at your sister or are you in a bad mood about something else? Does it really matter if your brother gets to use the computer before you do?

If you fight about the same things all the time, talk about it when you are getting along. See if there's a fair way to handle your problems. If you fight about where to sit in the car, take turns.

If you ever get really mad—so mad that you feel like hitting—go to another room. Calm yourself down by taking some deep breaths. Listen to some music. Watch something funny on TV or online.

Brothers and sisters argue. They just do. But if arguing turns into physical fighting, that's not cool. Neither is name-calling or saying mean things to hurt someone's feelings. Ask your parents for help before things get out of hand.

 I heard my parents talking about my older sister's curfew last night. What's a curfew? Should I have one too?

A curfew is a kind of house rule. It's a specific time that someone has to be back home. Parents use curfews to help keep track of when kids will be home—and to keep them safe. If you break a curfew, you might be grounded or lose certain privileges. Chances are, if your sister has a curfew, one day you will too.

Honesty and Trust

Q I saw my sister steal money from my mom's purse. Should I tell?

A Talk to your sister first. Are you sure she STOLE the money? Maybe your mom gave her permission to take it. If your sister did steal the money, give her a chance to tell your mom what she did. If your sister won't admit it, though, you should definitely tell your mom. Then let her handle the situation. You did the right thing, and now it's between the two of them.

Q I lied to my dad, and now he doesn't trust me. How do I win back his trust?

A By being honest, all the time. No matter what. Even when it's hard, tell your dad the truth. No little white lies either! Don't tell him you ate your broccoli if you put it down the garbage disposal. It will take some time to win back his trust. There aren't any shortcuts.

I accidentally broke Mom's special vase from her grandmother, and then I hid it. How can I tell her? I'm scared!

It will be hard, but tell your mom before she finds out. Explain what happened and apologize. Write a note if you feel more comfortable doing that. Accidents happen, but hiding the vase was wrong. Your mom might get mad. And she might punish you. But she'll get over it, and so will you. Offer to pay for the vase with your own money. If it can't be replaced, you could make your mom something special that reminds her of her grandmother. If an accident like this happens again, be honest about it right away.

Tip Clip

Trust is super important for good relationships. Being trustworthy is hard work sometimes, but it's worth it!

67

Family Changes

Q My mom and dad are getting a divorce. I'm so mad at both of them. How can they do this to me?

A It's totally normal to feel angry when your parents divorce. It's a huge change in your life, and you can't do anything about it. But remember that your parents don't want to hurt you. This is a decision between them. And it wasn't an easy one.

Sometimes life is hard. That's just the way it is. If time goes by and you still have a rough time dealing with the divorce, tell your parents. Try to be specific about what makes you angry and sad. Maybe it's that you have to live in two places now or that you miss Sunday morning pancakes. If you need more help, see if your parents can find a support group that's just for kids. Talking to a counselor or other kids going through the same thing can help you feel better.

Q My dad moved out, and I only get to see him every other weekend. What if he forgets about me?

A You're his daughter, and there's no way he could ever forget about you. You won't forget about him, will you?

Things will change, but you can stay connected if you try. Talk to your dad and figure out ways to stay in touch during the times you're apart. Have phone calls or video chats together. Write letters, e-mails, or texts. You can even play games together online. Save your school papers and go through them with your dad when you visit him. You won't see your dad at home every day anymore, but you can still be close.

How do I tell my friends that my parents are getting a divorce? It's embarrassing.

 Lots of families go through a divorce. There's no reason to be embarrassed. You didn't do anything wrong.

Confide in one or two close friends. Get used to the idea of having others know. When you're ready to tell your other friends and classmates, it's OK to keep it short and simple. If kids ask you questions you don't want to answer, explain that you'd rather not talk about it.

Tip Clip

Give yourself time to adjust to the "new normal" after your parents' divorce. It's a big change, but eventually you will get used to it.

My parents are splitting up, and my brothers and I feel like it's our fault somehow. How can we get them back together?

When parents split up or get a divorce, it's because they had problems. It's about them, not you or anything you did or didn't do. And no matter how much you might want to get them back together, it's not a good idea. That stuff is just between your parents. The best thing you can do is respect your parents' decisions and let them know how much you love them.

Part of the week I live with my dad, and part of the week I live with my mom. How am I supposed to keep track of all my stuff?

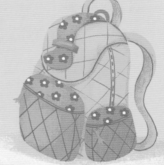

Lists can be a big help. Work with your parents to make a list of the things you will need to take with you every time. Make another list that's just for the current visit—things like library books, a sports uniform, or supplies for a school project. Before you leave one house, go through both lists to make sure you have everything. Keep your things together, so it will be easier to find them when it's time to go. If your parents are willing, you could get two sets of the items you need all the time, like toothbrushes or pajamas. That way you won't have to take them back and forth every time.

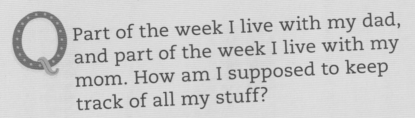

My dad remarried, and now I have an instant stepbrother. How am I supposed to treat a stranger like a brother?

Instant families aren't easy. Your new stepbrother may feel the same way. Treat him as you would a new friend. Play games together to break the ice. Find out what you both like to do. Pretty soon you'll get used to each other, and things won't feel so strange. Someday you might even become close enough to feel like brother and sister. If not, that's OK. You still gained a friend.

 My mom has a new husband and a new kid too. What if she likes her new stepdaughter more than she likes me?

You're still your mom's daughter, right? She still loves you. That didn't change. Tell yourself that you don't need to compete with your stepsister. Repeat when necessary! Try to get to know your stepsister. You are family now too.

When you and your mom are alone, it's OK to share your worries and fears. If you're too shy to come out and say it, write her a note. Make plans to keep spending one-on-one time with your mom, doing the things you like to do together. Be confident in your mom's love—and in yourself.

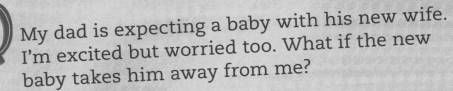

Q My dad is expecting a baby with his new wife. I'm excited but worried too. What if the new baby takes him away from me?

A Babies are a lot of work. Your dad will be busy and tired, and he might not have a lot of time for you at first. That doesn't mean he loves you less. As the baby gets older, things will get easier. Later on, if you need to spend more time with your dad, tell him. And when you see your dad having fun with the new baby, remember that he once did those things with you. Enjoy your new stepsister or stepbrother, and know that no one can ever take your place in your dad's life.

Q Since the divorce, Mom and Dad always fight when they pick up and drop off my sister and me. We don't like it. What can we do?

A It's hard to be caught in the middle. But your words may help. Tell your parents that their fighting bothers you. Ask them to stop.

Are the drop-offs and pickups happening at home? If so, could you meet in a public place next time, like at a restaurant or mall? If there are a lot of people around, your parents probably won't fight so much.

If things get really bad, talk to other family members or another adult you trust. You shouldn't have to deal with your parents fighting.

I really like my new stepdad, but I'm worried about hurting my dad's feelings. What should I do?

 When you're with your dad, don't talk a lot about your stepdad. You don't need to hide anything, but just enjoy the time with your dad. Your dad might feel left out sometimes, but you can't change that. Liking your stepdad is not being disloyal to your dad. The main thing is, your dad wants you to be happy. He knows that getting along with your stepdad is good for you and your whole family.

 I don't agree with any of my new stepmother's rules. Dad says I have to follow them anyway. Do I really have to?

Yes, you do have to follow your stepmother's rules. But think through why you don't agree with them. Is it really about the rules or is it more about your stepmother? Have an honest talk with your dad. See if you can come up with a plan you can all live with.

It can be hard to accept someone new in your dad's life. But there must be something good about your stepmother—your dad married her, after all. Give her a chance, and try to open up around her.

Ask questions about her favorite movies, TV shows, or sports teams. Share your favorite music or foods. Tell her something funny that one of your friends did. Things should get easier when you and your stepmother know each other better.

My grandma is very sick. She might die soon. How should I act around her?

 Let your grandma be your guide. If she wants to rest, sit with her and hold her hand. If she feels like company, you can talk, sing, or even read to her. She will enjoy hearing all about your life—your art project at school, the book you just finished reading, a party you're going to, and things like that. If she's well enough, make a memory book together.

Your grandma might look different than she used to, and that can be kind of scary. Be brave. She is still the same person inside— someone who is important to you and cares about you a lot.

If your grandma does pass away, it will be hard. But remembering all the good times you had together will help you feel better.

We moved because my mom got a new job. My old house was just down the street from my grandparents. My new house is three states away! How can I stay close to my grandparents now that we're so far apart?

 Just because you live far away doesn't mean you and your grandparents have to grow apart. There are lots of ways to stay in touch. Do your grandparents have a computer or tablet? You could video chat with them. That way you could show them your new puppy, play piano for them, or share your latest spelling test. If your grandparents aren't into technology, you can always talk to them on the phone. Writing letters can be fun too. Ask if you can visit them when you're on a school break.

Tip Clip

Don't take your loved ones for granted. Make the most of the time you spend with each other. The good memories you create will be with you the rest of your life.

I see my grandparents only once or twice a year. They don't have much to say to me. What can we talk about?

It sounds like you need to get to know each other better. Sometimes it's easier to talk to people when you're doing other things. Play board games, bake cookies, or make an art project with your grandparents. Go to a library or museum together.

If it's hard to get your grandparents to open up, try asking them questions about their lives. Pretend you're writing an article about them for the school paper or a class assignment. Ask to see old photos. If you're still having trouble, ask your parents for ideas to help you and your grandparents connect.

I really like hanging out with my aunt. She's super fun, and we do things that my mom and I never do together. Why can't my mom be fun like her sister?

It's cool that you get along so well with your aunt. But everybody's different. Think about you and your friends. Do you all like exactly the same things? Do you have exactly the same abilities? Maybe your aunt just has a more outgoing personality. Maybe she doesn't have as many responsibilities as your mom does. Maybe she has more money to do things. Plus, she's your aunt, not your mom. She doesn't have to do all the everyday things your mom does for you.

It's great your mom lets you spend time with your aunt. Next time invite your mom to come along. You might see a different side of her when she's with her sister.

Tip Clip

Gifts from the heart are awesome. Your parents, grandparents, aunts, and uncles will love getting anything from you, like letters, pictures, crafts, and baked goods. You don't need a special occasion.

Money

Q My parents give me an allowance, but sometimes I don't have any money left at the end of the week. Shouldn't my parents just give me money when I need it? My friends' parents do.

A Every family is different when it comes to money. Some kids don't get an allowance at all! Being good with money will become more and more important as you get older. And your parents know that. So if you learn how to make your dollars last now, it'll be so much easier later.

Set aside a couple dollars every week to build up your savings. Before you buy something, ask yourself if you really want it. Could you be just as happy without it? Keep track of your spending, so you always know how much money you have. And remember, little things add up a lot faster than you think!

Q I want to be on a soccer team. My moms say the uniform is too expensive and the team travels too much. How can I get them to change their minds?

A Being on a traveling sports team is a big deal. It affects the whole family, not just you. But there might be ways to make it easier. Could you carpool? Are there any businesses that donate uniforms to kids who can't afford them? Ask your parents to talk to the director of the soccer program to find out more.

If your parents still say no, you'll be disappointed, but don't let that change how you feel about soccer. Play as much as you can, wherever you can. Maybe when you're older, you can play soccer on a school team.

Q My dad has been out of work for a long time. Money's tight. It makes me worried, sad, and even a little mad too. What can I do to help out my family until he finds a job?

A The most important thing you can do is keep believing in your dad. Be positive. Tell him how much you love him, and encourage him when you can.

It might not seem like much, but simply doing what you're supposed to do can make things easier for your family. Keep up with your homework, and help out at home. Don't fight with your brothers or sisters. If you need something, it's OK to ask for it. Just try not to pester your parents about things you don't really need. They may not be able to afford extra stuff at this time.

Someday your dad will get another job, and then you can all feel good about how you pulled through this tough time together.

Tip Clip

You don't have to spend a lot of money to have a great family outing. See if your library offers discounted or free tickets to museums. Some libraries even show free movies. Parks, churches, and schools are other places to check for fun activities.

What to Say?

Q Our babysitter doesn't do any of the things she's supposed to do. She just sits around and talks to her friends. Should I tell my parents?

A Yes. Your parents are paying her to do a job, and she's not doing it. If they know what's going on, they can talk to her. Maybe she'll change her ways. If not, it might be time for a new babysitter.

Q A few months ago I moved in with my grandma. I don't know where my mom is, and I haven't seen my dad in two years. Everyone I know has a perfect family. How can I keep my new friends from finding out about my messed-up family?

A Your family might not be perfect—but you know what? No one else's is either. There's no such thing. Every family has problems that others don't see. And just because your friends seem to have it easy doesn't mean it's always that way.

You can't build friendships on lies. If you know your friends well and can trust them, you should tell them the truth about your family. You don't have to tell them everything—just what you're comfortable with.

Q I don't like the clothes my mom buys me, but I don't want to hurt her feelings. What should I do?

A It's tough, but just be honest and tell her they're not right for you. Be nice about it. See if you can return or exchange the clothes. Your mom will probably be disappointed at first, but she'll eventually understand.

The next time you need something, ask your mom to take you on a mother-daughter shopping trip. Or shop together online. Sometimes you'll get what you want. Other times you won't. But you're growing and will need a lot of clothes in the next few years. You'll have plenty of chances to figure this one out!

Tip Clip

When you feel a problem is too big to handle by yourself, talk to a trusted adult. We all need help at times. Sometimes the only way to get help is to ask for it.

Lunch Lines, Tryouts, and Making the Grade

Questions and Answers About School

What's one thing that nearly all kids have in common?

School!

School is a pretty amazing place. It's where you go to class, play sports and music, and hang with friends.

BUT SCHOOL

CAN SEEM

LIKE AN

OBSTACLE COURSE.

Every day you need to make a ton of decisions. Who should you sit with at lunch? Should you speak up or keep quiet? Will you study hard or do just enough to pass?

What do YOU want to know about school?

Q I feel like everybody stares at me when I ask a question in class. But if I don't ask questions, I get bad grades, and then I feel even worse! What can I do?

A Lots of kids are scared to ask questions in front of the class. They're afraid it makes them look dumb. But asking questions is actually a smart thing to do because that's how you learn! Besides, other kids might be wondering the same thing you are.

You can always talk to your teacher when other kids aren't around. Pick a time before or after school. If there's no time to talk, e-mail your teacher. Teachers expect questions and are willing to help out.

Q I'm not very good at reading out loud. How can I get better at it so the other kids won't make fun of me?

A You probably know the answer already: Practice. Read to your parents, grandparents, brothers, and sisters. Don't worry about reading fast right away. Take your time. If you come to a word you don't know, sound it out, syllable by syllable. Repeat it a few times, and keep on reading.

Go to the library and check out a book and the audio book with the same title. Then you can read out loud along with the audio. This is a good way to hear how words are supposed to be pronounced.

If it seems like letters are getting turned around, or you have trouble seeing clearly, tell your parents or teacher. They'll get you the help you need.

I get really nervous when I take tests. No matter how hard I study, I forget half of it as soon as the test is handed out. How can I calm down and do my best?

Get a good night's sleep the night before. It's tough to do well on a test if you're tired. And don't skip breakfast! Low-sugar cereal, yogurt, and fruit should hit the spot.

Right before your test, take slow, deep breaths. When you breathe deeply, your brain gets more oxygen, which makes it easier to think. Once you feel calmer, tell yourself, "I have studied, and I know the answers."

Tip Clip

Don't be afraid to ask your teacher questions. It's better to know something for sure than to guess. Besides, it's your teacher's job to make sure you are learning.

My teacher has us do a lot of group projects. But some kids don't do their share. How can we work together in a way that's fair for everyone?

 Start with a plan. As soon as you get the assignment, make a list of everything that needs to get done. Then divide the work evenly. Make sure everyone knows what he or she is supposed to do. Without a plan, some kids aren't sure what to do next, so they don't do anything.

If certain kids aren't doing their part, remind them what they're supposed to do. If they don't listen, ask your teacher for help.

I feel terrible when I get anything less than an A. My teacher and parents keep saying I shouldn't worry so much about my grades. But I can't help it!

Read pages 112-125

 It's great that you want to do the best job you can. But no one is perfect, and no one expects you to be perfect. It's the effort that counts. Really! So just do your best, and don't stress out. A few months from now, will you even remember a certain test or assignment? Probably not!

Q Twice a week, I get pulled out of my regular class to go to a gifted and talented class. Some kids think I'm showing off, but I'm not! Should I tell my parents I don't want to go to the classes anymore?

A Stay in the classes. You'll learn more and get to be around other kids who share the same interests. Don't brag or do anything to draw attention to yourself when you leave class or when you come back. Make a point of treating everyone the way you'd want to be treated. If kids who are giving you a hard time see that you're not looking down on them, they should lighten up.

Q I don't always do so well on homework or tests. I keep making such dumb mistakes!

A A lot of time, just slowing down will help. Don't rush through your homework. Double-check your worksheets or tests before handing them in. Did you answer all the questions? Are your answers complete? Is your writing readable? If you're still making lots of mistakes, talk to your teacher. He or she may have some ideas on how to improve your work in class.

Tip Clip

Grades are important, but they're not the whole story. Try your best, and you'll learn a lot. That's the most important thing.

Teachers

Q My classmates and I really like our teacher. How can we show her how cool we think she is?

A By showing her how cool YOU are. When you and your classmates behave well, she'll know that her students respect her. So get your homework done on time, and listen in class. That will make her feel great!

Q My teacher is going to have a baby soon, and a different teacher will be taking her place. What if I don't like the new teacher?

A Change can be scary. Give the new teacher a chance. Who knows? Maybe you'll really like him or her. Even if you don't, remember that it's for only part of the school year. Focus on the things you can control, like listening, doing your work, and trying your best. If you do those things, everything else will go more smoothly.

Q Some kids are mean to our substitute teachers. And some substitute teachers are tough. Is there anything my friends and I can do to make things go better?

A Teachers are supposed to be in charge of their classrooms. That's their job, right? So when kids act up, teachers might SEEM tough, when really they are just trying to keep things under control. Set a good example for the rest of the class by showing respect and following instructions. If your classmates do things they shouldn't, ask them to stop.

Sometimes I don't think my teacher is being fair to me. Should I talk to her or let my mom and dad take care of it?

 It's better to talk to the teacher yourself to see if you can work things out. Give her examples of times you think she was unfair. Your teacher will understand you better—and you will understand her better too. You'll feel proud of yourself because you solved your own problem.

If you don't feel comfortable talking directly to your teacher, ask your parents to get involved.

Tip Clip

Teachers are people too. They make mistakes. And sometimes your personalities just won't click. But if you're respectful no matter what, you'll get along better in the classroom.

Classmates

Q There's a new student in our class who is autistic. How are we supposed to act around him?

A With respect and kindness, no matter what his differences are. Then just follow his lead. Some kids with autism take a long time to warm up to others. Don't take it personally or try to force a friendship. Once you know him, you won't have to think twice about how to act.

Q A few girls are always saying mean things to me. How can I get them to leave me alone? And how can I keep the other kids from believing the awful things these girls say about me?

A Be strong. You know the truth and so do your friends. But you need to explain things to your teacher and parents. Those girls are bullying you, and that's totally against the rules.

Tell your good friends what's going on, and ask them to stick up for you with the other kids. But try not to worry too much. Your classmates likely know what's really going on.

One of my classmates wears a head scarf to school every day. I think it's really pretty, and I want to tell her. But my friends say I shouldn't, that it would be embarrassing. What do you think?

 Tell her. Wouldn't you want someone to tell YOU you looked nice? Besides, it might open the door for a longer talk. You can learn more about her background and why she wears a scarf. It's fun to learn about the things that make us different from one another.

 ## Tip Clip

Don't just stick to your usual friend group. Get to know as many of your classmates as you can. You never know when a new friendship might start up.

The boys who sit next to me are always goofing off. It's hard for me to pay attention to the teacher. How can I get them to stop?

First try asking them, in a nice way, to be quiet. If that doesn't work, talk to your teacher. There's a lot happening in a classroom, and teachers might miss things. Describe the problem and how it's affecting you. Once your teacher knows what's going on, he or she can help. Most teachers won't let on who told.

Sometimes the older kids at my school pick on the younger kids. Why do they act that way, and what can we do about it?

 Some kids tease because they don't feel good about themselves. When they make others feel bad, they feel more important. Some kids tease just because it's a habit—a bad habit. They don't even think about what they're doing.

Whatever the reason, you should stick up for the younger kids. If you had a little brother or sister, would you want someone treating him or her that way? Bullying isn't cool, especially bullying someone who is smaller and weaker than you. Tell a trusted adult so no one gets hurt.

Tip Clip

Being by yourself sometimes doesn't mean there's anything wrong with you. Learn to feel comfortable standing apart. Your confidence may even gain you some friendships!

Fitting In

Q I just got "dumped" by my group, and now I don't have anyone to hang out with. What can I do?

A Cliques are tough to deal with. It's hard to lose friends and feel left out. Look around—are other kids dealing with the same thing? Get to know them better, and then you won't feel so alone. Follow your interests. Get involved in group activities, like sports, choir, or theater. Get to know people one-on-one, and pretty soon it won't matter if you're in a clique or not. You'll have friends wherever you go.

Q My mom and I moved to a new city in the middle of the school year. I've never been "the new kid" before. I wish I could wave a magic wand and fit in with my new classmates.

A Being the new kid can be hard, for sure! Be yourself, and look for kids who are friendly or who like the same things you do. Join after-school activities or clubs. It might take a little while, but you will make new friends. Meanwhile, smile, and remember that you had friends before and you will have friends again.

Q A lot of kids at school don't talk to me because I'm in a wheelchair. It's like I'm invisible. How do I let them know that I'm just like them, except I can't walk?

A You may be the first kid they know who uses a wheelchair. They might be worried about saying the wrong thing, so they don't say anything at all. Make an extra effort to talk to kids while you're doing everyday school things. If you're comfortable enough, share with them why you're in a wheelchair. Be open to questions. They'll start to see that you're just like them.

Some schools have programs that teach kids about what it's like to have a physical disability. They even let kids try wheelchairs for themselves. Could you or your parents talk to your principal about doing a program like that at your school? You'd all learn a lot and have fun too.

 Q My friends all have something they're really good at in school. I'm never the best at anything. What's wrong with me?

A Nothing is wrong with you. Just because you haven't found your special talent yet doesn't mean you don't have one! Keep trying different things. And don't worry about whether you're the "best" or not. Do things because you enjoy them, try hard, and be proud of yourself.

In gym class, I'm always the last one picked for a team. I should be used to it by now, but it still hurts.

 It never feels good to get picked last. Talk to your gym teacher. Instead of picking teams, maybe kids could number off. Or maybe teams could be picked alphabetically. Both of these ways would save some hurt feelings.

Gym might be more fun for you if you work on your skills outside of class. Play team sports with your family or friends just for fun. Usually, the more you practice, the better you'll get.

Remember that not everyone is good at everything. Pay attention to the things you do well. Are you a good artist? Do you get good grades? Do you play an instrument or sing? Those things matter just as much as gym class.

 My mom drives me to school every morning and waits until I go into the building before she leaves. Sometimes she waves. It's embarrassing. I'm not a little kid!

 You're not a little kid, but you're HER kid, and she loves you. She probably can't help herself. See if she will compromise by parking a little farther away. Ask her not to wave. Instead, say good-bye in the car. That way both of you can start your day on a good note.

I like school, and I get good grades, but my friends think that's all I am—smart. I don't want to be called "Professor" or "Brainiac" all the time. I want to be cool! Is it possible to be both?

 Yes! You might have trouble believing it right now, but being smart IS cool. Be proud of your good grades! And of course you're more than your report card. What activities are you in? What kinds of things really interest you? Talk about those things with your friends. Be sure to ask your friends questions about their lives too.

If you're really hurt by the teasing, be honest. Tell them you don't like it. But remember, just because they call you "Professor" doesn't mean they don't think you're cool.

Tip Clip

If you notice someone who's alone, make a point of reaching out. You'll both feel great!

Q This year my school doesn't have enough money to let us take our yearly field trip to the zoo. My friends and I would like to help. What can we do?

A Talk to your principal, teachers, and parents, and let them know how important this field trip is to you. Brainstorm until you find a fund-raiser that's OK with your school. There are lots of ways to raise money. You could hold a bake sale, a car wash, or a silent auction. The businesses in your neighborhood may want to help too. You'll need to find one or two adults who are willing to be in charge. Once you've figured out a plan, you and your friends can spread the word and get lots of families to pitch in. Good luck!

BAKE SALE!

On days when I have a lot of activities, I have to stay up late to get my homework done. Then I'm tired the next day at school. What should I do?

 Activities are great, but nothing should come before your schoolwork. And being tired all the time is no fun. The easiest thing would be to take a good look at your activities. Which are the most important to you? Could you cut back on any? Give some up completely? Talk to your parents and see if you can work something out.

It'll be tougher if you don't want to give anything up. You'll need to start planning better. Make the most of the time you're given in class to get your work done. If you have big assignments that will take more than a day, break them down into chunks. Figure out which chunks you can do on which days. Try to do your difficult subjects first, when you've got the most energy. Can you do homework on the bus? In the car? Sometimes you might have to use some of your weekend time to catch up.

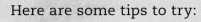

Q Every time I sit down to do my homework, I get distracted. How can I stay focused?

A Here are some tips to try:

Figure out the best time of day to do your homework. Do you like to get it all done as soon as you get home from school? Or do you need a break first? Are you more focused right before supper or after? Do you work better sitting down for a big chunk of time or for shorter times, with breaks in between? Once you figure out a time, stick to it every day. You'll train your brain to get used to the new homework schedule.

Get rid of the distractions you have control over. Turn off all the electronics (that includes the TV). Put away the new book you're reading or notes from friends. Clear your work space of clutter. Make sure you're not too hot or too cold.

Pick a spot away from the busiest parts of the house. Instead of working at the kitchen table, find a quiet spot someplace else. If you have a desk in your room, you could work there—unless being in your room is distracting. Ask your parents if you could work in their bedroom or office, or in a guest room.

Get all the supplies you'll need for your homework before you sit down. That way you won't have to keep getting up and looking for things.

Ask a parent or an older brother or sister to sit with you and read or do something quiet while you're doing your homework. Sometimes just being around other people who are focused can help you stay on track.

Do you know someone who is really good at getting homework done on time? Ask him or her for advice.

Q I tried out for a lead role in the school play, but I didn't get it. Instead, I'm one of the "extras." I don't think I want to be in the play at all now. If I'm not the lead, why bother?

A Being an extra will give you some good experience. It also means you'll have a better chance of getting a lead the next time you try out. Plus, being in a play is a lot of fun! It takes all sorts of creative people to put on a good play, not just actors. Someone has to build the set, manage the props, do the lighting and sound, and round up the costumes. And extras are more important than you think. What would a play be like with a mostly empty stage? Do your best, learn all you can, and keep trying for that lead role.

Q I want to be in the science fair this year. But it's the same day as my best friend's birthday party. How do I decide which one to go to?

A Did you say yes to one event before you found out about the other? If you did, you should stick with the first one. If not, you'll need to think it through. What's most important to you? Do you want to be at your friend's party or can you celebrate on another day? Can you work on science projects on your own or do you want to take part in the competition? Whatever you decide, remember that there will be more science fairs and more birthday parties to come.

Everything's a competition in my school. But what if I don't like to compete?

Some people like to compete because it makes them try harder. It makes them feel like they've achieved something. Other people don't do as well under pressure. But you should be able to find things to do that aren't based on winning or losing. How about band, choir, or theater? Take an after-school art class, join a book club, or volunteer at a local animal shelter. If you don't want to compete, don't. Be yourself.

 ## Tip Clip

Don't do the same activities all the time. Try something new. You'll get to know a different group of people, and you might discover a talent you never knew you had.

Lunchtime

Q Our lunchroom is so huge, sometimes I can't find my friends! Is it OK to sit by myself or with people I don't know?

A It's fun to sit by your friends at lunch. But whether your lunchroom is big or small, that's not always possible. So if you can't sit by your friends, sit anywhere you want. Talk to the kids next to you. Maybe you'll make new friends. If you'd rather sit by yourself, that's OK too. Be friendly, no matter where you end up. You might feel like everyone is looking at you. But don't worry. They're probably too busy eating and talking to notice who you're sitting with.

Q I have a bad peanut allergy. Some kids in school think it's funny to tease me about it. How do I tell them my allergy isn't a joke?

A Food allergies are serious. People can get really sick or even die from them. You should tell your lunchroom monitor or teacher about the teasing. Most school lunchrooms have rules about teasing and food allergies. Tell your parents too. Maybe the adults can come up with a plan to educate the whole school on how to handle food allergies.

Q My dad likes to draw cartoons on my lunch bag. I think they're pretty funny. But my friends think they're lame. Should I tell my dad to stop?

 A That's totally up to you. If you like the drawings and aren't bothered by what your friends say, let your dad keep drawing the cartoons. But if you don't want to deal with your friends' comments, ask your dad to draw on a notecard instead. He can tuck the card inside your lunch bag. Then you can still enjoy the pictures but share them only if you want to.

 Q The lunch lines at my school are so long, there's hardly any time to eat! What can I do?

A Could you bring a bag lunch? It's a little extra work in the morning, but you won't have to wait in line to get your food. You could also keep a snack handy, like a granola bar— something you can eat quickly on your way back to class.

Talk to your parents about the long-line situation. Maybe a group of kids and parents could get together and talk to the school staff. If enough people say something, the school may change the way it does lunch.

Getting Organized

Q I can't find things in my desk, and sometimes I have a hard time shutting my locker door. How can I be better organized?

A Go through your stuff often. Recycle old worksheets, throw out the garbage, and bring home the things you don't need at school anymore. If you make a habit of doing this, it won't take long at all. Once you're down to the things you absolutely need, try using shelves, bins, pouches, magnetic clips, and hooks. There are all sorts of things made to organize lockers and desks. Do you know kids whose desks or lockers are always neat? Ask them for advice.

Q I'm always the last one to finish a worksheet or a test. And it takes me forever to finish my homework. How can I make my brain work faster?

A Everyone's brain works a little differently. But the more you worry about how slow you are, the slower you'll be! So stop worrying. You do your work carefully, and that's a good thing. Kids who race through their work often make mistakes.

Q I daydream a lot in school. What can I do to make myself pay attention?

A Daydreaming is a problem for a lot of people. But it can be a good thing too. It means you have an imagination! When you are in school, though, you need to focus. Are there any patterns to your daydreaming? Is it harder to pay attention right before lunch? Maybe you need to eat a better breakfast. Then your energy will last until it's time to eat. Is it harder to pay attention near the end of the day? Maybe you need fresh air or exercise at recess. Do you daydream more in some classes than in others? If you tune things out because a subject is hard for you, ask your teacher for help.

Try wearing a rubber band around your wrist. When you start to drift, "snap out of it" by lightly snapping the rubber band.

Tip Clip

As you go through the school day, set aside the things you'll need to take home. Then you'll have everything you need by the end of the day.

Rules and Cheating

Q A couple kids on my bus were playing with a lighter. That's definitely against the rules. The bus driver didn't see. Should I tell? I don't want anyone to get mad at me.

A Sometimes you have to do the right thing whether or not anyone gets mad at you. If the kids on your bus are doing something dangerous, you should tell the driver. What if someone gets hurt? Wouldn't you feel bad if you didn't speak up? Once the bus driver knows what's going on, he or she can keep an eye on things.

Q Some kids are really rough on the playground. I'm afraid that I might get hurt. What can I do?

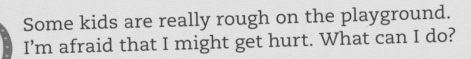

A Talk to the kids and ask them to tone it down. Or go play in another part of the playground, away from them. If that doesn't work, tell your playground monitor what's going on. Get some of your friends to go with you, so the monitor will see that the rough play is bothering other kids too. If the monitor doesn't do anything, talk to your teacher, principal, or parents.

I saw a boy in our class cheat on a test. I want to say something to the teacher, but what if he finds out I told on him?

 Go ahead and tell your teacher. It's the right thing to do. But wait for a time when you're alone and no one else can hear you. Or write your teacher a note or an e-mail. Describe exactly what you saw, and then let your teacher handle it. Most teachers won't let on who told.

Of course, the boy might guess it was you. If he gets mad, try to stay calm. Don't talk about it with anyone else—that will only make things worse. Whatever happens, remember that you didn't do anything wrong. He did.

Tip Clip

It's better to get a bad grade honestly than a good grade by cheating. If you're tempted to cheat because your parents are pressuring you to get good grades, talk to them about it.

Index

For Helena—NL

For Lydia—PS

Capstone Young Readers are published by Capstone,
1710 Roe Crest Drive, North Mankato, Minnesota 56003
www.capstoneyoungreaders.com

Library of Congress Cataloging-in-Publication Data
Cataloging-in-publication information is on file with the
Library of Congress.

ISBN 978-1-62370-218-2 (paperback)
ISBN 978-1-62370-474-2 (reflowable Epub)

Editorial Credits
Jill Kalz, editor; Juliette Peters, designer;
Svetlana Zhurkin, media researcher;
Charmaine Whitman, production specialist

Photo Credits
Alamy: Radius Images, 64; Getty Images: Don
Mason, 49, Jose Luis Pelaez, 27, 81, Jupiterimages, 89,
Sandy Jones, 34, Stockbyte, 46, SW Productions, 15;
iStockphoto: AlpamayoPhoto, 48, azndc, 72, CEFutcher,
82, digitalskillet, 58, ejwhite, 53, ferlistockphoto, 56,
GlobalStock, 90, Juanmonino, 62, 71, kali9, 18, 52, laflor,
33, LL28, 24, monkeybusinessimages, 20, RichLegg, 106,
Steve Debenport, 54; Newscom: Blend Images/Caroline
Schiff, 65; Shutterstock: Andy Dean Photography, 21,
AntonioDiaz, 86, bikeriderlondon, 23, 45, Blend Images,
10, 60, c12, cover, Denis Kuvaev, 37, Dragon Images, 28,
Elena Elisseeva, 4, 13, 40, Elena Vasilchenko, 84, glenda,
8, Jill Chen, 105, Kamira, 66, 100–101, kouptsova, 79,
Lisa F. Young, 95, lzf, 96, Margie Hurwich, 43 (middle),
Maria Bobrova, 38, Monkey Business Images, 50, 76, 92,
103, Odua Images, 43 (top), Patrick Foto, 74, Photocreo
Michal Bednarek, 51, Pinkcandy, 12, racorn, 99, rangizzz,
17, Smiltena, 14, Stephen Coburn, 30, Tyler Olson, 109,
wavebreakmedia, 68, ZouZou, 91

Printed in China.
092014   008475RRDS15

About the Authors

Nancy Loewen has published many books for kids.
She's a two-time Minnesota Book Award finalist
(*Four to the Pole* and *The LAST Day of Kindergarten*)
and the recipient of a Distinguished Achievement
Award from the Association of Educational
Publishers (Writer's Toolbox series). She holds an
MFA from Hamline University in St. Paul. Nancy
has two children and lives near Minneapolis.
To learn more, visit *www.nancyloewen.com*.

Paula Skelley is a blogger who writes about life,
loss, and pediatric cancer awareness. She holds a
BS in English and sociology and an MA in English
(creative writing concentration) from Minnesota
State University, Mankato. She is a mother of two
and lives in the New Hampshire Seacoast Region.

Nancy and Paula met years ago as English majors
at MSU, Mankato, and they have been friends ever
since. This is their first project together.

About the Consultant

John E. Desrochers, PhD, is a licensed
psychologist and certified school psychologist
who has worked for more than 30 years with
children and families in schools, clinics, and
private practice. He earned his doctorate in
educational psychology at Columbia University
and also holds graduate degrees in remedial
reading, behavior analysis, and marriage and
family therapy. John has numerous professional
publications and was recognized with a School
Psychologist of the Year Award by the National
Association of School Psychologists.

About the Illustrator

Julissa Mora has been a freelance illustrator for
more than eight years. She specializes in the
children's and tween market. She is best known
for her trendy tween girls, cute children, and
animal characters. Her work has been featured
by top industry publications such as *American Girl*
as well as by the award-winning toy company
Educational Insights. Julissa has been a part of
the Big Brother Big Sister organization, helping
to mentor her own little sister. Julissa currently
lives and works out of her home/studio in
Brooklyn, New York.